I0171739

Ladies, I Know Why You're Single

Ladies, I Know Why You're Single

by
ROMAY

ZAE Publishing, LLC
NEW JERSEY

Ladies, I Know Why You're Single

Copyright 2014 by Rodney Maynor
All Rights Reserved under
International and Pan-American
Copyright Conventions

Library of Congress
Cataloging-in-Publication
Data is available

ISBN: 978-0-615-95744-9

Cover design by ZAE Media, LLC
Printed in the USA

Distributed by ZAE Publishing, LLC

Ladies, I Know Why You're Single

Ladies, I Know Why You're Single

Ladies, I know why you're single. That may not be a problem for some of you.

However, after loosely conducting an extensive survey over the course of some 30 years, I've learned that the majority of women, regardless of culture or financial status, have desires to be married, or at least be in a relationship. Needless to say, the single woman to man ratio is far from equal, thus leaving many eligible women without a male counterpart while having strong desires for one. To say that there's a simple solution is the furthest thing from the truth.

#LIKWYS

So often in women's social circles, you'll hear that 'men just don't get it', and while this might be true, it's still a bit questionable. We must first diagnose exactly what "it" is before we point the finger at who doesn't have it. In much the same way that you couldn't pick which shell that the ball is under in a game of shuffle unless you know that there's undoubtedly an existing ball.

Well, this is about the "it" that men allegedly don't get and why that ultimately drives women crazy enough to pull their hair out and worse, pull his out. Whomever hair gets pulled out, it's sure to say that a couple that doesn't see eye to eye will land somewhere in the unfortunate realms of checking off that dreaded box on forms and online. That box that seems to be bigger than the rest of the boxes that need to be checked on a form. That box that makes you question your life, presently and where it "needs" to be in the future. Yes, that box, ladies. The "SINGLE" box.

I'm not sure which one matters most, being single or the reason why. What I do know, however, is that it's very hard to see the forest when you're amongst the trees. Simply put, I doubt that any woman that finds herself single and of a certain age, while turning her nose up at the very men that she's attracted to, due to her past, can really understand where the blame lay. You can make an

3

appointment with your therapist or you can stage a night out with a group of friends that share the same ideals as you. You can even join an online group and post anonymous rants. Needless to say, there will never be a source and salvation more credible than the very thing that you deem to be the problem. A man.

Well, ladies, I'm sorry to tell you that what you may think is the problem,
really isn't. Ladies, I know why you're single...and in these pages, I plan to point out all the reasons why, so that you may be aware of your flaws, your virtues and those things that drive men absolutely crazy, in a good way.
Naturally, you will not agree with everything here, but even if there's one

thing that you can identify with, then there's room for change. So proceed with caution from here on and share your views, for your relationship status depends on it.

#LIKWYS

CHAPTER 1:

CONFIDENCE

I think it's necessary to start off with the most important thing, because it's this very thing that will open your ears and mind to accept what you may need to change about yourself to win. A confident woman is like an ice cold beer in a sports bar with a bunch of hot waitresses to a man. He will pay close attention to her every move and remember her every word uttered. She could say that she's running late and it will glide from her tongue in such a heavenly way as to make him want to stop traffic to allow her to pass so that she gets back on schedule.

I recall a woman telling me of her situation with a guy that she was seeing at one time. I immediately asked, at the onset of our conversation, why wasn't she still seeing him? Her response was simple. She had lost her confidence. The very same confidence that she'd had when she caught his eye. She began her story by telling me that she'd met him in federal prison, of all places. He was an inmate that had spotted her while she was visiting her Uncle and he was engaged in a visit with his brother. When she looked him square in his eyes as she walked to the vending machines, he knew that she was sure of at least one thing. He seemed too sure of another.

Weeks later, after he'd asked her uncle about her and telephone conversations were shared between the two, she felt compelled to pay him a visit. She woke up early that morning to get prepared to show this guy exactly why he had no business being in such a place and what was on the outside awaiting him. The day before, after work, she'd fulfilled an appointment with the Chinese lady for a fresh Brazilian wax, so everything was nice and smooth down there. Her outfit was to her liking, her makeup was flawless and she smelled like heaven. He thought so too. So much, that as soon as he walked into the visiting room and was allowed to have the one of two kisses during visitations, he wasted not a moment. And throughout the time of the visit, he couldn't keep his eyes and hands off of her.

That visit and the many that followed until he was released and home with her went well. He grew closer and more attracted to her. It was like each time that he'd see her, was the first. Not much changed in those regards when he was there at home in her bed every night either. At least, not at first. For about a year or so, he made love to her and sexed her in ways that she hadn't imagined. It was as if he couldn't get enough of her. Whether she was just in from work or on her way out the door, he wanted her totally. He'd come in from the gym, from work, from anywhere and would be all over her. Sometimes he didn't wait to come in; he just did what he had to do wherever they were. She loved it.

Then one day she noticed something about her relationship. They were having sex less and she had unconsciously grown okay with it. He would try and she would make excuses or just be too tired. This was also around the time that she realized that it was time to go shopping for some new clothes that fit. Most of her work clothes were a bit too tight for a business environment and she began to feel self-conscious around her fellow employees. She told herself that she would take her guy up on his offers to come to the gym with him at least once a week...if the offer was still on the table after the 10th time that she'd refused or ignored it. More time passed, less action between the two of them occurred and she stopped going out to lunch with co-workers and friends. She'd even stopped wearing makeup and doing all the things that she used to do to make herself so desirable. Those monthly waxing's were history.

It didn't take long for her attitude to change about things. She always felt left out when she opted out. She always felt the need to defend herself, even in simple situations. She grew distrustful about everything, including her relationship. Before long, her guy couldn't take it anymore and he suggested that they part ways. Since then, she said that she'd been on dates and managed to be in a few short term relationships that suffered because of her sour views on life and herself, but was willing to do whatever's necessary now to have a healthy long term relationship.

After reading about this woman, it should be clearly evident as to why she lost her relationship and had troubles forming new ones. Her confidence had slipped to a low and she'd projected her own internal feelings of herself onto those around her, namely, her man. Ladies, there's a saying that goes: You

#LIKWYS

will keep him the same way that you got him. This simply means that if you got the man that you want by grabbing his attention with your looks, your intelligence or your smile, then it's the right thing to continue in that manner. You just might gain a few pounds and you may not wear the same hair style that you once did. Granted, he's not expecting you to be runway model ready every day, all day, but he wants to know that he's still with the woman that stole his heart from day one. That woman that was confident enough to look him in his eyes and know that she was what he needed. Don't have confidence in yourself, ladies, and you're sure to be single for a long time coming.

CHAPTER 2:

TOO ARGUMENTATIVE

Women assume a lot of things about men, especially when she's mad at him. The top assumption is that 'men simply want a woman that just sits quietly without a word'. Well, there's a small bit of truth in that, but with stipulations. You see, men want women that have a lot to say, but the key is in knowing when and how to say it. Oftentimes, ladies, when you've come across the opportunity to let a man know that he's done something wrong in your eyes, it seems as though your intentions are to tattoo it in his brain forever. That one statement that tells him or explains to him of how disappointed you are in his actions becomes an argument filled with lyrics from a broken record. I can say with certainty, that being so argumentative will first lead to a man becoming disengaged from the conversation. Then he will eventually become disengaged from the relationship altogether.

I had a friend that was married for some years. He and his wife shared 2 kids, 2 cars, an average sized house and a dog. From where they'd come, they were doing well. He worked hard to put them in a great place financially since she was so used to being catered to with all her every wants and desires. You see, she grew up in the rougher part of her town and had just one brother and three sisters.

All the sisters, including her, we're drop dead gorgeous with bodies that drove men crazy and every player and hustler from the neighborhood wanted to choose. Their brother was well respected, but had the responsibility of also being a father figure to his younger sisters, since Dad was long gone. Split that in half with his job and sometimes one or two of the most persuasive guys got through to his beautiful sisters. They didn't stay around long.

By the time the youngest of the 4 sisters was just turning 18, big brother was headed to the Army. This left the sisters vulnerable to the persuasions of whatever came their way. The 3 older quickly were lucky enough to land in the arms and care of boyfriends that seemed respectable. The youngest wasn't so lucky. She was recruited by a young hustler, to be his main girl. He bought her everything she needed, wanted and dreamed of. She drove nice cars and wore expensive jewelry. Until he was one day arrested and taken from her. That's when she met my friend.

Money was running low and she was in a training program to get her certification in nursing. My friend instantly took her into his life and only requested that she finish her schooling.

By the time she'd graduated, they were planning a wedding and a year later, she was pregnant with their first child. He figured that it was time for them to move into a situation that was better for her, him and the children, so he brought a house.

That's when everything changed. Although all was fine on the home front, she began to snap at him whenever he asked her simple things. He guessed that she needed space during those times, but she would find him to start new debates and arguments. When his friends stopped by and he escorted them to the basement after greeting her, she found a way to come downstairs to join into conversations simply to debate his every word. His friends would go silent, until eventually they stopped coming by altogether.

Four years passed and she grew more argumentative about everything that came from my friend's mouth. She even argued about his thoughts. Then one day he asked for a divorce. It was a simple divide, where he gave her everything. The house. Her car. The joint bank account. Everything. He only required his peace of mind and the opportunity to live as he should have with her. In no time, she was single and I'm sure you know why.

Ladies, don't think for one minute that a man gets enjoyment out of a battle or constant debate with his significant other. He wants to know that you have your own thoughts and opinions, but that you both share a common destination. This is what attracted him to you beyond the first date. Ignore that and you won't just find yourself single and without a relationship, but you'll find yourself feeling alone within the one you're still in...for now.

#LIKWYS

CHAPTER 3:

FORECASTING

A man can always tell a woman that will more than likely be a problem from a mile away. She's the one that makes it of the utmost importance to let you know what she's not going for because of what she's been through already. It doesn't need to always begin or accompany a rolling of the neck or some finger snapping, wrist twisting gesture, but it will certainly begin with her telling a man about a past situation. The ending of the statement or story, whichever he can stand to bare hearing, will close with her asking him if he's into such behaviors....."because if you are, then we're not gonna work". At that point, a man can take one of two steps, but he will surely only have one thought. Let's deal with the thought first.

When a woman decides to be "preventive" in a relationship, there's only one way that a man can think, initially. She will tell him that her ex left the toilet seat up after using the bathroom and he will automatically, without even thinking about it, empathize with her. He won't want to see her go through such experiences ever again. He will start thinking of ways to counteract her feelings of disappointment and also the act of doing it himself. Needless to say, we are all human and mistakes come with the turf, so if there ever comes a time when he dares to leave the toilet seat up because he's half asleep, stumbling through the darkness at night to use the bathroom, then trust that she will feel as nostalgic about that toilet seat being left up as Janet Jackson performing on stage at the Super Bowl. She will snap. And he just might leave.

I remember a woman that I'd met some time ago. She was very well established with beauty and brains to match. We met in an after work lounge. You know, one of those places that's nestled in a downtown area, deep between corporate offices and municipal hangouts. I saw her seated alone at the bar. We locked eyes for all of one second and I figured that was a sign for me to engage in conversation with her. I offered to buy her a drink. She accepted, but alerted me that she was in fact waiting for her significant other to arrive. I understood and put her dirty martini on my tab anyways.

We began a conversation that lasted for close to an hour and still her partner hadn't arrived. She was working on her third dirty martini by then and her honesty had begun to take the place of her being so uptight. She told me of how inconsiderate her guy had been lately. She told me how he was always the gentleman in the beginning of their relationship, listening to her, catering to her and never being late for anything, as that was her pet peeve. Being late was something that she couldn't deal with, since her past relationship before him was never on time. She told me of a particular time when she'd scheduled an appointment for them to get massages at 6am, but told him that it was 6pm, just so that they wouldn't be late. When they arrived and he'd seen the doors to the spa closed and the lights off, he was livid. He was probably boiling when he found that she'd already made hotel arrangements for them at the hotel where the spa was housed in. Her rational was that at least they wouldn't be late now.

#LIKWYS

She went on to tell me how he had never bothered to be on time since then. She hoped that it was a passing phase and that he was only a tiny bit bothered by the fact that her proactive arrangements had forfeited a deal that would have come from a business meeting that he didn't attend. I listened and watched her fidget with her cellphone and check her watch constantly as she told me this story. She asked for another martini and who I was there waiting for when she and I met. I told her that I was just passing time away before I was due to meet a date soon. She seemed a bit bothered by that and grabbed her cellphone to make a call. She listened to something on the other end of the call, but never spoke. When she took the phone from her ear, she downed the last martini and told me that her man didn't answer when she'd just called him. I thought about how he probably would never answer her calls nor see her again. Based on what she'd told me, it seemed like he'd had enough and finally took it upon himself to end it. I felt bad for her.

So I motioned to the bartender for the check, because it was nearing my time to go, as I didn't want to be late for my engagement. I didn't have reason to be. I asked if she'd be okay driving and she assured me that she was fine. She planned to give him a few more minutes to possibly show up, before she caught a taxi home. I gave her a few words of advice in leaving: I told her that all men, when we approach a new relationship, want to know what the last guy did wrong, so that we don't rub you in that way also. It doesn't have to be an ongoing conversation that lasts throughout the relationship. It would be best not to pepper your first dinner with that conversation either. It makes like an interview for a position that he'd love to have, but in a company that he might not be so fond of. With that, in due time, he'll be so resentful from hearing about your past relationships and what you won't stand for from him because of it, that he'll be ready to call it 'quits', leaving you single yet again.

I asked if she was okay again and she responded that she was, so I paid the tab, wished her well and walked out. I thought about her and many women that I've known like her, with those same forthright expectations and pressures, for days after. I liked the seclusion and the lighting in that bar, so I found myself there again some weeks later. Surprisingly, the woman that was waiting for her partner was there too. I offered to buy her a drink and asked her how things turned out the night that we'd met. She looked straight ahead into the mirror where the bottles of liquor were strategically arranged, at our reflection and told me that her man never showed up that night and when she arrived at home, his few things that he kept there were gone along with the house keys that she'd given him on the counter. Again, I felt bad, but it didn't surprise me much. At that point, she turned to look me straight in my eyes and asked if I knew why she couldn't seem to stay put in a relationship. I paused a minute, while thinking of all of the hopeless, homeless and heartless men that would overlook a woman forecasting her past relationships onto them just for a warm bed at night, and I replied, "Yes, I know exactly why you're single"....

CHAPTER 4:

CREDIT CARD SEX

There's not a human being, woman or man, walking on this earth that doesn't wish to be correct in everything that they do. Nobody aims to do wrong. We set our sights on the right thing and hope that nothing steers us from our path. However, let something or someone misguide us, and oftentimes we believe that there's no returning to that righteous road. That's just us being the humans that we are.

#LIKWYS

Needless to say, there's a whole other type of thing happening when it comes to women and your wrong doings. For some strange, but understandable reason, women feel that it's perfectly fine to commit any treasonable act within a relationship as long as she can follow it up with mind blowing sex. Some women don't even believe that it needs to be mind blowing. She simply thinks that he should be happy that he's getting something that's so good and desired by him nonetheless. So no matter what wrong she's done, said or plans to do or say, sex with her gives her the credit to get away with it. This may have all of you scratching your heads, adjusting your wigs and wondering what problems are there in that. I say none...if you're ok with providing a commodity that may not always be in stock or in season. Other than that, you can be sure that he's one day going to grow tired of sex between you two being regarded as your personal credit card and start making plans to leave.

Credit cards get many people in trouble. We buy things when we know that we have no money to at that moment. Some of us rely on credit. Actually, it's credit that keeps our economy running. Swipe a card and you're free to go about your business as if the issue of no money never existed.

Well, this is the problem with you ladies in relationships and it drives men crazy

#LIKWYS

when we get to the point of realizing that
you're simply trying to shut us up until
your next act of treason. Some of us
realize it sooner than others, while many
men will prove to be deaf, dumb and
blind to things that just may be right in
their faces. If that's the case, then I have
added advice here for you, ladies. It may
be time to trade him in for someone
that's a bit more conscious of the world
and your relationship, enough for you to
be proud to show him off.

I once knew of a guy that I frequently
ran into at the barbershop that I held
appointments at. He would be at the
barbershop when I came in and he would
still be there when I left. He was in no
rush, letting other patrons in the chair for

haircuts and shaves before it was his turn. I found that to be strange, so one day I asked him about it. "Why do you hang around here all day and let people take your turn in the chair?" I asked. He told me that there was nothing to go home to since his wife doesn't cook on weekends and she's usually out until late. I didn't want to pry, so I simply shrugged with a tilt of my head and nodded, feeling unsettled inside. I immediately began to wonder why this man before me was so docile and accommodating to what his wife was putting him through. Before I could muster up the heart to say anything else, he asked me if I had time. I checked my watch and realizing that I had a few minutes before I had to leave in order to make it on time for my next stop, I removed my hat and relaxed a bit to hear him. He told me that he and his lady had been together for about 2 years and how great it was in the beginning. I nodded, while thinking that all relationships are well polished at the start. He continued and told me about how incredibly sexy his lady was. How she dressed well and even chose the right perfume to compliment her body's natural aroma. He almost overheated when he mentioned how hot she was in heels, which she almost always wore. So I wondered what the problem was with him and his relationship to this seemingly perfect specimen of a woman. He went on to tell me that she was well aware of his admiration of her beauty

and made sure to use it to her advantage.
I was puzzled and it showed on my face.
At that point, this man became a bit
lively and animated, as he told the

remainder of his story. He explained
how his lady, despite her beauty, had
grown into an inconsiderate and
disrespectful person. She'd go out with
friends at night and show up at home just
before daybreak, without a call or
anything. When he was watching a game
on TV, as he did on most Sunday
afternoons, she'd make it her business to
come into the room and have a loud and
distracting conversation on her
cellphone. On many occasions while
they were together in their apartment,
she'd made or ordered lunch for herself

without checking to find out if he wanted to eat as well.

All this and he continued to maintain the relationship that he felt slighted in. So I asked why, with an even more puzzled look on my face. He sighed and told me that with each wrongful deed that she engaged in, there followed him telling her how it rubbed him wrong and her ultimately rubbing him some more, physically. She seemed to believe that sex made everything better and allowed her to do the things that she was doing wrong. Sort of like using a credit card to buy what you know you can't afford.

I asked him what he planned to do about the situation, because I could sense that this man was troubled. Without much of a pause, he seemed to be looking through me when he said, "I just did something about it". I asked what he meant and just then, his eyes locked back with mine and he told me that for the very first time that he's ever been

able to confide his situation with someone like now, he's come to realize that the relationship with this woman isn't what he wants. With that, he said that he would be ending the relationship that day.

As you know, credit card spending doesn't just buy you what you want. It also buys you time. In this case, I think that the woman used sex as her credit card to buy time until her man found out that she couldn't pay the bill of her wrongdoings. In the end, she may have had the offers on the table that kept her out until the early morning hours from time to time. Needless to say, she found herself single and without that good man that most woman plea that there's not enough of. Overuse of "credit card sex" to offset bad behavior will put even the most responsible person in debt and this, ladies, is why you're single.

CHAPTER 5:

SOCIAL BROADCASTING

It makes every man feel good to know that his lady is holding him in high regards. However, there's a thin line between giving a man his props and telling all of his personal business. With social networking and media being the highest priority on the list of communication these days, a man is more likely to know the status of his own relationship by way of Facebook, Twitter or Instagram, before he's learned of it from his own partner. For some odd reason, women feel compelled to share with the world, the ups, downs and issues that plague their relationship. What you don't realize is that not only are the listeners and readers entertained by your childish behavior, but they're also placing judgment on you, the relationship that you're in and the man that you're including in your posts or conversations. Meanwhile, he's growing tired of defending himself, not only with you, but also with the public.

A good friend of mine repeatedly ran into some bad luck. I like to say that it was a bad luck streak, since it lasted over the course of 2 years. His significant other was a bit addicted to social media. The first thing that she did before rolling out of bed in the morning was log onto Facebook to see what had been posted and commented on while she slept the past few hours away. She spent her days at work and the commute home in heated online social debates and discussions that resulted in her walking in the door at home with any given emotion. By then, my friend would also be walking into their place, cellphone in hand with his eyebrows bent and a headache to add, due to what he'd read about himself online. From the private conversations and moments with his lady to what they'd eaten the night before, he saw it and what everyone had to say about it.

It was quite embarrassing to see that people that he either barely knew or didn't know at all, making comments on his personal life that she had shared like it was entertainment news. It was her birthday, that year that they would break up. She made certain that he and the world knew exactly what she wanted for her special day. She picked the dress, the shoes, the jewelry, the restaurant and the position that she wanted to have sex in. "Vera Wang, Jimmy Choos, fully loaded Pandora bracelet, a bottle of Veuve Clicquot on her table at the 40/40 Lounge & Restaurant, and doggy-style, so that she could feel all of him inside of her". She posted that entry online at 6:02am, as she turned the water on to shower that morning before work. Everyone went wild about her expectations. Women said that she deserved it. Men said that she wanted too much. Other men and women said that if her man didn't get it for her then they would. She loved the attention almost as much as she would love the gifts.

The end of the workday couldn't come fast enough for her. She'd gotten up to 100+ comments on her post and the responses were still rolling in. She grew more excited with each new comment. My friend was excited too. He couldn't wait to put that incredibly gorgeous smile on his lady's face for her birthday. It's what made him so attracted to her in the first place. He tried not to pay attention to her post that he looked at from time to time that day. It was just too much to read and he knew that he would be disturbed by some of the comments, as he always was. Tonight was her night, so he was going to aim not to get heated by her online broadcasts. So he focused on the evening. After work, he would make a few stops and give her time to get home and begin getting ready for their night out. It was a Friday.

He came in about an hour after she did. He held 2 bags in his hands, both with gift wrapped boxes inside. She was in her robe, applying her make up. She looked great. He kissed her neck and took in her sexy scent, whispering "Happy Birthday to my lady". She giggled. He pulled the shorter end of the belt on her robe to reveal her well moisturized, naked body. She was flawless and he wanted a pre-birthday celebration sampler. She told him that they could wait until later tonight when it would be even sweeter than it already is. He got off his knees, from in front of her and grabbed the bottle of champagne that he bought home to have their own private toast with. As she went through the bags to greet herself with the garments that she would wear for the evening, he popped the first bottle of Veuve Clicquot for the night. It startled her and she jumped while letting out a short but cute, high pitched scream. He poured them 2 glasses and made a toast to "great times and timeless beauty that stands before me". She blushed. He got undressed and showered as she made herself into the queen that he saw her as.

When he came out of the shower, she was just finishing up with her accessorizing ritual. She was stunning from head to toenail polish, except she was frowning a bit. He asked if all was ok and she said that it was, but he noticed the tone of her voice and the continued frown on her face as he dressed. He tried to pour himself another glass of champagne, but the bottle was empty. She'd drank it all while he was showering. During the ride to the restaurant she barely spoke, but that didn't keep her from paying a lot of attention to her cellphone and updating the details of her night, minute by minute, on her social networking profile. By the time they'd arrived and were awaiting their turn for the valet to park their car, she wanted to tell him the cause of her change in attitude, but was too angry to say a word. However, she wasn't too angry to post about it. He hoped that she understood and was thankful for what he'd done so far for her special day.

After all, that was his job, she thought. Nevertheless, there was something missing. He hadn't included the Pandora bracelet and charm set that she'd requested and posted about on Facebook and twitter days before. So now her posts reflected her "inconsiderate boyfriend that never gets anything right" and she was spoiling her own birthday celebration. What she didn't know was that he had the bracelet in his pocket and wanted to give it to her at dinner.

She refused to take any pictures and had more interest in looking around at others than at her date. My friend grew restless and figured that a restroom break would give his disgruntled lady a few minutes to regroup, so he excused himself. While he was in the men's room, he took the opportunity to check Facebook on his cellphone, to see what she might have been saying about the evening since that's where she always reported her business at. Not surprisingly, she had been reporting everything about her birthday, from the time that they'd awakened and the amazing sex that they'd had before showering together. He already couldn't understand her necessity to share their private moments, but now her attitude made it unbearable. Then, ten posts from her and a few hundred comments later from her online friends, there she was insulting him to the world, for not doing what she felt was right. His blood boiled and he thought about all the time and consideration that he'd put into trying to make her birthday special. He thought about the Pandora bracelet, loaded with charms, which he had in his jacket pocket at the moment. He also thought about how ungrateful she was, along with being so terrible enough to broadcast what should have been shared and solved privately, between them. It was that very moment that he realized that he knew that his relationship was hopeless. So he finished up in the restroom, paid the tab for the food that they never had a chance to enjoy and left car fare on the table for her to get home. And just like that, she was single.

Ladies, you might say that my friend was wrong to have left his lady behind at a restaurant alone, but think for a minute. His lady had been leaving him alone in the relationship for some time now. She had taken it upon herself to do what she saw fit without his consent from the beginning and she knew that he didn't like it. Now she had to pay the price of it.

If you don't wish to understand anything else about this story, then understand this: Men love to be appreciated, noticed for his values and spoken of for great deeds, but there is absolutely NO MAN that wishes to have his private life and business shared with others that will ultimately judge him for it, to themselves or in public. Be the culprit that does this in your relationship and ladies, I can assure you that you will find yourself single.

#LIKWYS

CHAPTER 6:

EVERY OTHER WOMAN

This is the "denial chapter". I've coined it that because not just a few women will say that it doesn't apply to them. All of you will say out loud, right this very minute, that you aren't the least bit jealous about your man being friends with other females. If you dare to admit that you are jealous, then you're quick to rationalize the reason or reasons why. You might say that he has a bad track record of past. You might say that you know how women are these days. You might even take the preventive approach

#LIKWYS

by befriending the other woman that's in
question, just to keep your eye on what
you might think is going on. Whichever
reason that you find your man and
another woman to be a distrustful
combination, you have to realize that
sometimes your eyes can be so open that
you miss what's right in front of you.
This is a sure way to find yourself
single.

I had a female friend at one time. She
was extremely beautiful and had all of
her ducks lined up nicely. In other
words, she was well established in every
way. She drove a nice car, had an
amazingly fun and well paying job, nice
home and a handsome, hard working and
accomplished man by her side. All of her
friends approved of and some envied her

relationship, because she and her man looked so good together. They would go out as a couple and get stares of admiration from other couples and single men and women alike. She loved it, just as long as she was close by to assure that those other women wouldn't make any advances. She'd lost many nights of sleep due to this.

As I've stated, my friend's guy was handsome. He received just as much, if not more, attention from women while he was out alone or at work. A smile always came with every transaction and conversation that he engaged in with a woman throughout his workday. He wrote it off as proper work behavior and continued on with his work, 5 days a week. Almost everywhere that he went for lunch, sometimes meeting up with his lady, my friend, he enjoyed a discounted check and flirty eyes. It felt good to know that he could make so many people smile, as his life was in order thus allowing him to smile as well. Those days that she was there, he was on pins and needles. There was also Facebook.

My friend's man wasn't a Facebook junkie by far. He occasionally logged on to "like" a few people's posts and post a few of his own opinions, beliefs and wise words. His true reason for initially creating a profile was actually to find her, since they hadn't been in touch since high school and everyone from their class could be found there. He'd had a crush on her some 15 years ago and it amazed him to have her in his life now. If only he could fix her jealousy and misguided speculations. She would find malice in each of his online female friends' comments and hold him accountable for it. He could barely stand it, as it embarrassed him when she acted on her speculations. It made him reluctant to have and reconnect with female friends, as he didn't want them to share any of that experience.

A few years after they'd gotten together, their class reunion had arrived. They both agreed to go so that everyone could see them and admire how good they looked as a couple. All she could think about was the aftermath-the day after, when everyone posts and comments about who and what from the night before. She knew that she and her man would be crowned as best looking couple. They always were. To be honest, the comments had started earlier this time around. He posted that he 'couldn't wait' for the reunion and everyone went crazy with comments and "likes". My friend "liked" it too, because she couldn't wait also. However, mainly because she wanted to receive alerts whenever someone added another comment to the already never ending thread. So when the night before the much anticipated class reunion came, she spent her hours combing through the profiles of every female on her man's Facebook post that dare say what she defined as flirty. She was making mental notes to prepare for any looks, comments and whispers that might be cast the next night.

Then there was the infamous wink. Yes, the one that's made with the ";" and ")" keys together. She saw it, placed at the end of frivolous comment, but she was sure that it meant something. She did what she'd already done some 30 plus times already. She traced the comment all the way back to the profile of the woman that it belonged to and made the assumption that this could be someone to pose a threat to the relationship between she and her man. The final straw for her was that this woman's relationship status was said to be "single". Boiling with accusation, she reached over to her man and woke him from his sleep. She asked him what was going on between him and the "winking" friend online and his disbelief of her waking him from his sleep for such nonsense was shown on his face. That disbelief and the accusation that caused it trickled over to the reunion the following night and she found it hard to leave her man's side. Whenever she did take a moment to engage in conversations of her own or to grab a drink at the bar, her eyes were locked on her man. He felt it and before the end of the night, she couldn't stand it anymore, so words were exchanged between the two of them.

The event was over at 2am and so was their relationship. He refused to continue to tolerate her accusations and mistreatment of their relationship, which ultimately found its way to embarrass him in public. She rode home in silence, shocked at his words and received the confirmation that he was serious when he simply dropped her off and went to his own house to sleep. She was now single.

Ladies, its already enough on a man to be the one for you to respect, admire and be turned on by. However, it becomes a confusing equation for him to figure out how not to be to other females. Just because he's being cordial, that doesn't mean that he's involved or interested in her. As women, you have an incredibly ridiculous desire to be attracted to the everything that you don't wish for your man to be. You share gasps of air when you see a shirtless picture of your favorite actor or entertainer, but you don't want to allow your man to remove his shirt for fear that other women may want what's yours. Nobody's saying to share your man by any means at all. What's yours is yours and you should appreciate that. However, wrongly convincing yourself that every woman that your man comes in contact with is a potential for dismantling your relationship will make YOU the other woman that'll be looking in from the outside, and single too.

CHAPTER 7:

VICTIMIZED

How many times have you heard a man in conversation, speaking about how wrong his ex did him? Not many, I'd bet. How many times have you heard another woman, or maybe yourself, recounting how dirty a past love did you before you just couldn't take it anymore? Almost always? Okay, lets agree that most of the time its a woman who's hearts have been victimized in a broken relationship. However, ladies, that doesn't mean that there's no cases where a man is being stepped on and taunted by your ease in making yourself seem like the victim in every situation. Do this in a relationship and guess where you'll find yourself? Yes, you got it...single.

There was a couple that lived in the same building as me once. They lived on the floor just below me and oftentimes one or the both of them would ride the elevator up to our apartments with me. I lived on the 16th floor, so that gave us enough time to exchange acquaintances and pleasantries as something more than strangers. After some time, they'd grown very comfortable around me, enough to do a lot of touching and other intimacies in my presence. I wondered how far they would go while I was so close, there in that small elevator. Nevertheless, with acts of love comes acts of resentment.

In the midst of what had to be an argument, the couple would walk into the building and share an elevator ride with me. I'm sure that had I been another tenant or visitor in the building, they would have refrained from their outward behavior. However, since I wasn't a stranger and they knew me well, they continued to argue without pause. Well, she did. The man would try to get a word in, but she would always over talk him with words and volume. I guessed that he didn't really want to make a scene, so he awaited his turn to talk, that of which I'd never saw happen. As the elevator doors closed and they walked down the hallway to their apartment, I could still hear the young lady yelling. I wondered what this poor guy was constantly doing to piss his lady off so much.

So, one particular evening on my way in from a meeting, as we were sharing an elevator ride up, the couple was noticeably quiet. I did what I would regularly do by asking how they were. The young lady half smiled and said that she was fine. That must have been the chance that the guy needed, because he took in a deep breath and asked me if I've noticed how she's always yelling and fussing with him as they're coming in the building together. I nodded without saying a word. He asked me if I noticed that he never had any opportunities to say anything back. I was a bit afraid of how she might react to that question, so I remained silent, knowing that he understood. He then told me that her reason for being so upset and seeming like the victim of some situation or treatment that he was responsible for came from his questioning her about her attitude towards him lately. He'd been in this relationship with this woman for a year and a half, accepting her issues of accusing him, broadcasting their private business to the world and thinking that sex would make it all go away. Needless to say, there was a problem whenever he brought up these issues and how they affected him. She would break into a tirade and shut him down by making it seem as though he'd wrongly accused her much the way she said that every man did in her past.

He couldn't take it and I saw his breaking point standing there in the elevator with us like a fourth person.
When the doors opened she stormed out, mumbling obscenities at him for finally having a chance to tell his side of the story and having someone to hear it. He looked at me and shrugged his shoulders. The elevator doors closed and seconds later I was stepping off to walk down the hall to my apartment. I turned to him first and asked him what happens after such a blow up. His response was simple and plain. He told me that he would go down to their apartment, pack as much of his things that could fit in his

car and he was gonna leave. For a minute I felt bad for their situation and wondered if things would have gone a bit different had I not been in the elevator. With that, he wished me well and the elevator doors closed.

Ladies, it may seem like a small thing for your man to allow you to vent your frustrations while he stays quiet. You may think that he has no issues or dislikes for anything that you do within the relationship. You may believe it to be his job not to feel any kind of way about anything at all. Needless to say, it's not fair. He should definitely have a shoulder for you to lean on and an ear to listen, but neglecting to understand that you're in a relationship with another

#LIKWYS

human being that deserves to be heard could be damaging. Overshadow his chance to share those things with you by forever reminding him of your woes and it could be the end of your relationship, much sooner than later. Simply put, victimizing yourself as a means to soak up all the attention in a relationship is a one way ride to being single.

CHAPTER 8:

PERIOD TIME OUT

Everyone wishes to be able to do two things at once. Some of us want to do more than just two things. Society today tells us that it's necessary to have the ability to multitask at work, as well as, in our home life. We get hired to do one thing to find ourselves doing many more, and for the same reward and recognition. Then we go home to our children and significant others to juggle being parents, cooks, referees, friends and a great lover. It seems like there's never a chance for us to say "time out".

#LIKWYS

Ladies, however, you do possess the great ability and gift to throw up the capital "T". It's a God-given gift that continues to be presented to you on a monthly basis. You may not see this as a gift, because of the pains associated with it, but you'd be surprised to know how much a man would love the built in opportunity to tell the world to leave him alone. The problem with this gift of yours though, is that you'd like for everyone and all things to stop moving as well. Well ladies, that's not reality. Unless you're pregnant, your menstrual cycle will come and it is a part of your life. The key word there is "YOUR". In a relationship, it's very important to your future to understand that just because you are immobile and sometimes confined to the bed for days, that doesn't mean that your partner is also. Expecting him to press pause on his activity 12 times a year, to match your inactivity isn't fair and could certainly add up to the end of that relationship.

Years ago, I had a friend that was seeing a young lady that seemed to be a nice catch. She was drop dead gorgeous, knew her way around the kitchen and maintained a solid career. She always invited me and my significant other over for dinner to be overwhelmed with her undeniable cooking skills. We would leave their place stuffed and fulfilled with great conversation. They seemed perfect and looked forward to one day soon, being married and having a kid or two. My friend only wished that she didn't shop for shoes so much. He didn't mind working an extra hour overtime here and there to support her habit. He just wondered about the space to put them. I explained to him that he'd better learn fast that ALL women love shoes. After that, he probably should start doing a little shopping of his own, for a bigger place to store her shoes.

We laughed at his woes and made jokes at his expense often. His lady even joked about it and figured that her payment to him was to allow him out with the guys for beers, pool or whatever at least once or twice a week. While we would be having beers at a local sports bar, she would text him pictures of her latest shoe love, with "LoL" attached as a message. It was always funny to see his expression when those messages came through. What wasn't funny was how my friend would behave for at least one week out of every month. He would grow very quiet and distant until ultimately he would disappear, only to resurface some days later as if he'd just been released from a punishment of some sort. It happened often, but I couldn't put my finger on why until we'd made plans to attend a basketball game to see both our favorite teams play against each other in a newly built arena and he couldn't make it.

We'd purchased the tickets almost a month in advance. We were excited and looking forward to this night of trash talking that always came from our teams rival. Plus, they would be playing for the first time, in a fresh and much talked about arena that had one of the greatest sports bars nestled inside of it. My significant other had friends over and said that she'd maybe tune into the game on TV if that's what her girlfriends wanted to do. The only friend missing from the gathering was my friend's significant other. I asked why she wasn't there, only to be told that she was having "women's issues" and chose to stay at home tonight. I guessed that was fair enough and went on to call my friend to see if he was ready to head to the game. His response was a bit low and inaudible, so I asked him again. He then told me that he wouldn't be going to the game because his lady had cramps. I told him that I understood and hung up the line, but couldn't make sense of any of it to save my life. I just didn't know what his lady's menstrual cycle had to do with him, unless she'd missed it. Then it all came tumbling down on me. The understanding of his change in attitude and the silence every few weeks, I mean. Like clock work, I didn't hear from my friend for a few days and he wasn't as animated when we spoke. I took that as a sign not to ask any question or divulge what I'd come to understand. Needless to say, he initiated the conversation with a recap of the game that I'd went to without him a few nights before. We talked about a few key plays and I paid him the $20 from a small friendly bet that we'd made on the game. He then told me that he wasn't too sure if he could take it anymore. I asked him what he was referring to before I assumed anything out loud. I was sure that he was going to tell me that he made up a "no new shoe" rule for his household. I was prepared for a laugh. What he did say, however, was that he was fed up with being on his period for 3-5 days every month. I looked in horror, but just listened. He said that the past year of his 2 1/2 year relationship has been a predicted and well timed hell as he was expected to stay still while his lady was immobile during her menstruation. He told me that while it was okay initially, because it allowed him to get a few things done around the house, he now grew restless, regularly refraining from any activities without a reason of his own.

I had no real advice to give him on the matter, since it would be his choice in whether he was willing to continue dealing with a situation that he already seemed disappointed by. However, I did refrain from inviting him out since I didn't t keep track of his lady's personal business. Nevertheless, he would show up for a beer from time to time, but with a whole different attitude. I'd notice him check his phone after a text came through and I awaited the smile that would be on his face, but there was none. It had faded. A few months later, so did his relationship.

Ladies, you can't change what you are, but we all can change how we are. By now you have experienced having your period enough times to know exactly how to handle yourself in every situation. Well, almost every situation. It may seem ideal for your man to not be active whenever you aren't. To some of you, that would mean that he cares. Again, you should be fair in what you propose to your relationship and the other person in it. I can assure you that there's no man in the world that looks forward to waking up in the AM to shave. That's a daily ritual for some of us. Now could you imagine him waking you out of your sleep everyday to stand by and watch him shave and pluck hairs from his nose? I'm sure that you'd take issue with that. So ladies, I will be firm in saying that if you're expecting your man to share your period with you, along with the "time out" that comes with it, then you should also expect to be single soon.

#LIKWYS

CHAPTER 9:
DRESSING THE PART

I'm a firm believer that in order to make the proper impression, then one must dress the part. This holds true for a relationship just as much as it holds true for an interview or business meeting. I'm sure that you wouldn't attend a business meeting in your pajamas, unless you were privileged to work from home and had the luxury of video conferencing. Even then, you might need to have your face made up. These days, a lot of women forget how to dress the part for the role that they want, all the while labeling themselves as such. You see it on social media all the time, a female calling herself "wifey" or a "good mom" as she's dressed in heels meant for a stripper, a tight dress that barely covers her lower body whenever she adjusts it to hold in her upper body.

Ladies, this isn't the chapter that I tell you not to be sexy or make yourself up to be attractive for your man, partner or significant other. This is the chapter where I will advise you not to dress as if you're doing a photo shoot or profiling for Instagram. Looking as if you're prepared to twerk is fine when only your guy can see and enjoy it, not when others can lust and anticipate the chance that you might reveal something of interest. Dressing like you're on the market might be cute, but I can assure you that after he's confirmed that you two are an item, then he won't be voting for that attire anymore. He'll want someone that he can respect enough to bring home to his Mother...even before he gets the chance to.

Once upon a time, I shopped in a particular high end store that catered to your every need and desire. If you wanted coffee or tea, it was made available as you shopped. Caviar? No problem. Bar-B-Q ribs with a side of macaroni and cheese? No problem. I especially enjoyed bringing others there with me to share what it was like to be well taken care of. However, I liked more, the conversations that the owner and I engaged in during my visits alone. I would phone him ahead of time and he would have my favorite scotch there, on a tray with 2 glasses when I arrived. We would leisurely drink glasses of liquor as we exchanged stories of what our lives consisted of at the moment.

He was a very well dressed man and believed that the most stylish component to an outfit was being neat. You would see him moderately dressed in jeans and a t-shirt and know that he'd spent time and money finding just the right fit and brand to suit him. Then there was his wife. She was just the opposite, always dressing in what she thought was the latest trends at all times. I could sense the discomfort in him whenever we were all out and were in earshot of other guys that made claims about things that they'd love to do with her. I didn't see anything wrong, as it was just confirmation that he'd made a great choice in a woman. Then again, maybe I was impartial because I wasn't affected by it. A few drinks usually took his mind off things.

Those were the weekends that led to the dreaded weekdays when my friend's wife would engage in domestic duties in her signature attire, nonetheless. She went to the grocery store in heels and leggings. She went to parent/teacher conferences in tight jeans, shirts with plunging necklines to show off the double Ds that he bought her and of course, heels. Although still young, their kids were embarrassed and often defended themselves against the other kids and the school staff alike. My friend's wife still saw no need to tone down her wardrobe to reflect her being a mother and a wife.

She did wonder, however, why after 10 years of marriage and 2 kids, why she'd only met my friend's parents twice. Whenever she'd ask him, he would go silent to avoid hurting her feelings with the truth. His parents learned before the wedding and upon first meeting my friend's wife, that she didn't look the part. They played their positions at the wedding, but refused to be in her presence thereafter. Christmas and birthday gifts for their grandchildren came by mail.

By the time the kids were 9, my friend's wife had gotten the hint and filed for divorce on the grounds that she felt out of place in their marriage. She never changed her attire, because she never saw anything wrong with it to begin with. As I was shopping for a suit some years later, my friend mentioned to me that she'd been married and divorced 3 more times. I deduced that her subsequent marriages didn't work for the same reasons since she was otherwise a fair woman. Needless to say, she couldn't find herself any other way except single.

#LIKWYS

Ladies, not all men will take issue with your dress code. Not all children will be embarrassed by your stilettos. You may not even get a blink from the occasional lusting guys out in a club. Nevertheless, no man, child or their grandparents for that matter, will want to claim you if you're dress code hinges on being the next pin up in Maxim or STEEL magazine. Its very important to understand which outfit goes with which situation. Fail to do so and you could be forever thrust into a life of being alone.

CHAPTER 10:

POWER COUPLE

There's a title that women like using to describe highly publicized relationships, including their own. Power Couple. I've witnessed celebrities, politician's and sports couples, all characterized as these power couples. There's nothing much wrong with that as long as you're making powerful strides in light of your relationships security on every level. The sad part is that most of you that are placing the "power couple" label on your relationship partake in behaviors that are just the opposite. Instead, you're in search of every way possible to be the most powerful IN the couple. Its sort of understandable why you ladies might be engaging in such behaviors within your relationships.

If you take a poll of 10 women above the age of 35, you will come to realize that 9 out of 10 of them have been in a relationship or several that have left her with a sour taste in her mouth that can still be smelt in the air as she speaks. The key to that statement isn't that she's been through a situation that rubbed her wrong, but more about the fact that she's carrying it with her. These are the same women that take preventive measures in every relationship that they might encounter moving forward by being controlling. This, in your minds, is the only way to ensure that things go the way that you wish for them to. I'm sorry to tell you that you're wrong. Try controlling the relationship or the man in it with you and you will without a doubt end up single. If this doesn't hold true, then the man that you are in the relationship with needs to be controlled and therefore begs for your situation to be questioned.

I have a close friend that suffered an unfortunate situation some years ago. He had gotten himself involved with a bad bunch of guys that were doing some insider trading on Wall Street. He ended up doing 5 years in federal prison, with a $3 million fine. Between the case and helping his loved ones to stay afloat while he was away, he was wiped out financially when he was released. He considered trying his luck on Wall Street once again out of desperation, but I temporarily talked him from that ledge. It was his longtime girlfriend turned fiancé that convinced him to live a life void of criminal activity for good. Needless to say, there were some stipulations. She'd been writing to him and making visits to see him while he was away, so she believed that he owed her his life, in a sense. Add to it, the failed attempts at moving forward in other relationships before now and she had a plan and compensation package all put together for herself. What she didn't consider was that her man wasn't too likely to feeling forced nor obligated to anything that resembled the time that he'd just done in federal prison. My friend was very appreciative for everything that we all aimed to do to make his integration back into society as smooth as possible, but he cringed every time his lady had another way that he should do things to fit the way she wanted their relationship to go and be seen by others.

She told him where he should work, as opposed to the place that he sought employment. She told him how to spend his money, when it was his money that took care of them for years. She made an issue of whom he was friends with, because she feared that his unmarried friends would influence him to never propose. It was as if she didn't trust in his judgment with anything anymore and wanted to have the power to make things fit her own agenda without his say so.

One day as I was visiting their home, my friend asked if I would stay for dinner. He planned to grill some steaks, chicken and a few other things as we drank a few beers. I jumped at the idea and didn't dare to think about putting my coat on to leave. His lady was in listening distance and seemed excited enough to inject that it would be better if my friend cooked the food inside to avoid getting bit by bugs. She went on to tell us how she would also be able to taste the meats to be sure that they were cooked to her liking. I could see my friends expression changing with every word uttered from her mouth. I saved the situation from becoming volatile by insisting that we grill the meats outside on the patio to stay out of her way as she made the salad inside the kitchen.

We were lucky that time, but I later found out that my friend's fiancé wasn't just controlling. She was very demeaning in how she addressed him whenever she didn't get her way. Whether it was in person, over the phone or in her online rants, she had an abundance of names to call him. I would have never believed it was happening if I didn't have the opportunity to hear their conversation once. He was at my home and had taken a call from her in another room for privacy. I know now that it was from shame. I could clearly hear her screaming at the top of her lungs on the other end of the phone while he tried to get a word in. My friend was being bullied in his own relationship and I knew what would soon happen. Weeks later, he confessed to me that he'd began seeing someone else. He explained how this other woman knew all about his situation at home and posed no issues to his peace of mind. She actually was very accommodating and listened as he shared with her his desires for things to work with his fiancé and him. I told my friend that he couldn't continue on with both women and urged him to either make things work or do everyone involved a favor by ending the relationship. One week later, he ended the relationship between his fiancé and himself.

In this day and age, women have been empowered with titles and positions such as CEO, top earners and head of households. While this might not be much of a problem to the crusade for equal rights for women, it could very well be a hindrance to the wellbeing of a relationship. A woman that doesn't know how to be a woman in her relationship is doomed to be in a bad one. The woman that knows how, but refuses to play the position of the female in that relationship can look forward to being alone sooner or later. Being with someone in a relationship requires respect and consideration to run alongside the love that you should have for that person. There's no race to be won and no competition to outshine your mate in. Needless to say, ladies, if you think there is then you should not only expect to be single. You should accept it.

CHAPTER 11:

THE ONE WAY

There, you have ten reasons and examples not to follow. At some point in your life maybe you've been guilty of at least one of them. There are millions of stories and experiences that could teach and be your guidelines, but without an understanding of your mistakes, they will remain to be just an earful. Everybody makes mistakes and whether it's one or many, it's up to you to learn from them without repeating so that you ultimately end with the prize that you wish for.

#LIKWYS

Surely there are more examples that I would love to share for the sake of entertainment, but I'm certain that if you've come this far along in this book then by now you have a clear understanding of what's wrong and what's right when it comes to relationships. As simple as men seem to be, where pleasing them is concerned, he's much like a woman with his list of unacceptable behavior. Feeding him and keeping him pleased sexually can very well mean nothing if he's stuck with any of the things mentioned in the previous pages of this book. Nevertheless, it's not always about what the man likes or dislikes.

I've heard women profess on numerous occasions that there's power in their ability to say when the sexing is going down. Surprisingly enough, I agree. The problem, however, is that there's no waiting period being exercised anymore. While we live in such a fast paced world today, nobody shows any patience for anything. It's almost like the possibility of no tomorrow is embedded in everyone's minds upon meeting each other. On any given night with any given female, a man can have a one night stand. These days, you ladies are initiating it too. It's said that men are dogs, so imagine how a dog behaves when he wants what you have. He will sit, lay down and even bark if you say so.

#LIKWYS

Ladies, your availability is the key that opens the door to a successful relationship. No relationship will be without disagreements, but most of the time it's you that will make yourself available to him for things to be back on the right track. It's you that always makes time to do whatever he invites you to do. It's you that is always available and he realizes that.

You want that man to marry you, or show an interest in you that feels like it? Start first with the understanding that regardless of how laid back or attractive he may be himself, man contains an inherent nature to lust over the woman that interests him before and once he's come to love her. Although women love to have sex just as much as men, give in to him sparingly and he will give in to you totally. Bottom line, the dream girl is the one that he dreams about having all the time.

I believe that one great jewel deserves to shine in the presence of another. With that said, it's necessary to shine light on the fact that you are a spectacular breed. A jewel. Ladies, as much as you may believe that it's the man that shapes the relationship, it's you that truly has the power. There are things that he may not tolerate in a relationship that could ultimately lead to the end of it just the same way that he may be a bit much to deal with as well. The key to that is in identifying those things that you don't like and can't be fixed, so that you can make room for what does. Place and maintain a high value of yourself and ultimately this will even bring you a better man. Try this and you can be assured that you'll soon be checking off a different box on those forms and social networking statuses. Taken.

#LIKWYS

#LIKWYS

Rodney Maynor is the self published author of *Myths, Memoirs and Confessions of an Ex-Felon*. He writes under the pen name of RoMay. During 2008, Rodney co-hosted and produced *A Black Man's View*, an often times comedic internet show on YouTube that addressed real world issues. He is also the founder of *STEEL Magazine* & co-host /producer of *Raw STEEL Radio* (the brainchild of the originally named, *SWeT Radio*), a weekly internet show on Blogtalkradio. Rodney, CEO of *ZAE Publishing LLC,* was

#LIKWYS

the primary subject in a documentary entitled *Blacks In NJ* , produced in September, 2009.

Rodney has also co-produced *The Solitary Pen*, a stage play based on *Myths, Memoirs and Confessions of an Ex-Felon with a local playwright.*

#LIKWYS

#LIKWYS

#LIKWYS

#LIKWYS

www.ingramcontent.com/pod-product-compliance
Lightning Source LLC
Chambersburg PA
CBHW060328050426
42449CB00011B/2698